CAMP
CARE♥A♥LOT

**A Fun, Comprehensive K-5 Program
Where Coping and Social Skills are
Taught and Practiced in a Unique Setting**

Written By Lisa Eck, M.

Camp Care-A-Lot

Softcover ISBN: 978-1-57543-313-4

COPYRIGHT © 2016 MAR∗CO PRODUCTS, INC.
Published by Mar∗co Products, Inc.
214 Kale Road
New Bern, NC 28562
1-800-448-2197
www.marcoproducts.com

Graphic images © http://123rf.com

PUBLISHER'S NOTE: This publication is sold with the understanding that the publisher is not engaged in rendering psychological or other professional services. If expert assistance or counseling is needed, the services of a competent professional should be sought. Care has been taken to confirm the accuracy of the information presented and to describe generally accepted practices. However, the author, editors, and publisher are not responsible for errors or omissions or for any consequences from application of the information in this book and make no warranty, express or implied, with respect to the contents of the publication. Mar∗co Products, Inc. is not responsible for the content of websites referenced in our publications. At the time of this book's publication (2016), all facts and figures cited are the most current available. If you find an error, please contact Mar∗co Products, Inc.

Mar∗co Products, Inc.
214 Kale Road
New Bern, NC 28562
Phone: 1-800-448-2197
Fax: (215) 956-9041
http://www.marcoproducts.com

To purchase additional copies of this book or request a catalog, call our customer service department at 1-800-448-2197.

Printed in the U.S.A.

CONTENTS

A Message From The Author

Camp Care-A-Lot was developed to help school counselors meet the increasing needs of students with a decreasing amount of time available to do so. Classroom instruction time has become so focused on meeting academic goals that social-skills lessons are not given the attention they require. *CCAL* offers social-skills lessons such as identifying feelings, dealing with anger and worry, and developing a positive mind set and coping skills.

Students participating in *CCAL* eat lunch with the facilitator for 10 weeks. The group can be large since the students are divided up into smaller sized "cabins" consisting of 3-6 students. Best of all, the program can be adapted to fit your needs. For several years, I lacked the ideal setting. I lead *CCAL* in a hallway, and was able to reach students with valuable life lessons.

I have students who begin to ask for *CCAL* the first day of school. There are students who have been in the program for several years and gain something different each year based on their current needs and development.

Let's Get Started! Checklist

☐ Determine a location in your building that is available during lunch time. (A multi-purpose room with multiple tables works best.)

☐ Create a schedule based on your schedule and classroom lunch times. (For example: Tuesday–Grades 1, 3, 5 and Thursday–Grades K, 2, 4)

☐ Give yourself time between groups. Do not schedule back to back lunches.

☐ Send home permission slips.

☐ Promote the program during morning announcements, classroom lessons, etc. (Explain the purpose of *CCAL*. Make the program sound fun, but also be sure the students understand that you will be presenting serious topics each week. Emphasize that *CCAL* is not a time to socialize with friends.

☐ Talk with cafeteria workers about having the students come early for their lunch time.

☐ Talk with custodian about using trash cans, cleaners, etc.

☐ Share a schedule and a list of students who will be attending *CCAL* with their teachers.

☐ Gather lunch materials such as napkins, forks, spoons, straws, etc. to avoid students having to leave to get materials.

☐ If possible, announce that the groups are meeting each day on the morning announcements. (For example: Attention "campers"! Grades 2 and 4 meet today for *CCAL*. Teachers please allow the students who are participating in the program to leave a few minutes early for lunch.)

Other Suggestions

The following four suggestions were found to be beneficial as the *Camp Care-A-Lot* program was being developed.

1. Offer a time for parents to come in and share with them what the students will be learning in *CCAL*. The best turn out occurred when a light breakfast was offered and children were allowed to join their parents.

2. Take 10 minutes during a staff meeting to promote and explain your program to teachers. This will help them to understand the goals of the program and the need for students to be released early for lunch. If they see what *CCAL* offers their students, they'll be more willing to help!

3. Go with the flow! Some groups are going to be more challenging, especially kindergartners. Don't be hard on yourself if you don't accomplish everything each week.

4. Be aware of students who are impeding the group's process. Don't let one student ruin it for the others. If a student is negatively impacting the rest of the group, discuss this with him/her at another time. Be specific about the importance of following procedures. Explain that if the student chooses to continue to behave inappropriately he/she may have to leave the *CCAL* group.

CAMP CARE♥A♥LOT
Is Coming Soon!

Dear _____:

The *Camp Care-A-Lot* program gives children an opportunity to talk in small groups about issues they have concerning many different situations. The group's participants and I will eat lunch together one day a week for ten weeks. Children will learn coping skills such as identifying feelings, learning what they can and cannot change, and how to instill positive self-talk into their daily lives.

Children who could benefit from participating in *Camp Care-A-Lot* are those going through challenges in their lives (divorce, separation, new stepfamily, lack of a parent figure, loss of a family member, moving, etc.) or a child might just need some extra encouragement to feel successful. *Camp Care-A-Lot* is also a great experience for children who are dealing with teasing and bullying.

You and your child are also invited to a *Camp Care-A-Lot* breakfast to inform you about what we will be discussing each week and how you can encourage your child to get the most out of the group experience. The breakfast will be held on:

_____ from _____ to _____

If you would like your child to participate in *Camp Care-A-Lot,* please return the permission slip below by _____. Please indicate if you plan on attending the breakfast. If you have questions please call _____ at _____.

Thank you,

_____
SCHOOL COUNSELOR

✂ ....

_____   _____   _____
CHILD'S NAME   GRADE   TEACHER'S NAME

Please check what applies to your child:

☐   Divorce or separation
☐   Death and bereavement
☐   Other life changes, adjustments, or encouragement: _____

_____   _____
PARENT/GUARDIAN SIGNATURE   DATE

#_____ will be attending the *Camp Care-A-Lot* breakfast on _____.

"Cabin" Groups

As signed permission slips are returned, begin to group the students according to their needs, personality, and age. Placing students in the appropriate "cabin" groups is very important to ensure they get the most from the *CCAL* experience. Limit each "cabin" to six students.

Although it is important that *CCAL* is fun, it is also important to avoid it becoming just a "social event" that students experience with their friends. To insure this, confer with teachers to find out more about a student's situation and which students shouldn't be sitting by each other.

If you do not have a room with multiple tables, you can still assign the students to seats. This eases the anxiety about where to sit each week and still allows students to be around those who are experiencing similar situations.

If necessary, discuss privately with the students any concerns they have about where they are sitting. Adults aren't always aware of conflicts between kids. However, assess the situation before making a sudden move.

Below is an example of a "cabin" group assignment sheet. The assignment sheets should be placed in plastic frames and put on each "cabin's" table. A template is provided on the CD.

Weekly Supplies

Gather the following list of supplies before *CCAL* starts and have them available throughout the entire program.

☐ Small flashlights and batteries for *Flashlight Feelings* (page 13 or CD)

☐ Markers, pencils, pens, extra paper as needed (see specific weeks for details)

☐ Attendance chart (page 15 or CD)

☐ Table seat assignments

☐ Lunchroom supplies such as straws, napkins, utensils, etc.

☐ Cleaning supplies and and trash cans

Flashlight Feelings

WHEN: *Flashlight Feelings* is played at the beginning of each session once all of the students have arrived and are situated in their seats. This activity should only take 3-5 minutes.

WHY: This activity enables students to build rapport and trust with their "cabinmates," and to learn from each other by sharing their life experiences. *Flashlight Feelings* is such an important part of the CCAL experience because this is when the "campers" learn to identify and share their feelings and to empathize with one other. You are simply the facilitator.

WHAT: The students share how their week is going with other members of their "cabin." For example, someone may say: "I am excited to see my Dad this weekend, but I'm worried he will have to work and I won't get to see him very much."

HOW:

1. Select which student in each "cabin" will begin the activity by asking a question like: "Who is wearing orange?" or "Who's birthday is next?"

2. Tell the students that the person with the flashlight does the talking, then the flashlight is passed to his/her right.

3. The other students are "good listeners."

4. Instruct the students to use their inside voices.

5. As the students share how their week is going with other members of their "cabin," circulate among the groups to ensure students are behaving appropriately, being encouraging, and listening. Offer help with the conversations and encourage the students to role-play their responses. Ask the students how their week is going and have them respond by making a *thumbs up* or *thumbs down* motion. You may also choose to have the students answer the question by saying "great," "so-so," or "terrible." Students may say "pass" if they choose not to answer. Each student could also share one reason why he or she is feeling that way.

6. As *CCAL* progresses, encourage the students to use feeling words in their sharing experiences.

Frequently Asked Questions

What should I do if a student wants to quit the group?

Find out why he/she does not want to attend. Some reasons may include:

A friend is not in *CCAL* and the student does not want to eat lunch without his/her friend.

The student is feeling uncomfortable because of his/her own situation. I had a student who did not want to reveal that he was being permanently removed from his parents' custody. *CCAL* was hard for him. We worked together, and I encouraged him to stay in *CCAL* and just to listen to the other "campers." He ended up having a great experience!

What do I do if a student wants to join **CCAL** *but doesn't have a signed permission slip?*

Follow your school district's policy as to what permission is needed for a student to join a counseling group. A phone call can be made to the student's parent/guardian if you feel *CCAL* would benefit him/her**.**

What do I do if I have to cancel a group session?

Situations may occur that prevent you from keeping your intended schedule. Assess your students needs and the groups needs and plan accordingly. Try to alert the students ahead of time when you know there will be a change of schedule.

Camp Care-A-Lot Attendance Chart

GRADE LEVEL: _____   DAY: _____   TIME: _____

NAME	TEACHER	REASON	WEEK 1	2	3	4	5	6	7	8	9	10

PROCEDURES AND RULES

Facilitator's Goal:

To have students understand the group's procedures and routines

Materials Needed:

For the facilitator:
- ☐ Table seat assignments
- ☐ Small flashlights for each student group/cabin
- ☐ *Attendance Chart* (page 15 or CD)
- ☐ Lunch supplies
- ☐ Trash can and cleaning supplies
- ☐ *What's In A Backpack?* (optional sample, CD only)
- ☐ Interactive whiteboard (optional)
- ☐ *Camp Care-A-Lot Bingo* calling cards (optional activity, pages 28-29 or CD)
- ☐ Scissors (optional activity)
- ☐ Camp Song: *I'm Going Wildlife Watching* (optional activity, page 30 or CD)

For each student:
- ☐ *What's In Your Backpack?* (page 21 or CD)
- ☐ Crayons
- ☐ *Camp Care-A-Lot* Bingo card and markers (optional activity, pages 22-27 or CD)
- ☐ Camp Song: *I'm Going Wildlife Watching* (optional activity, page 30 or CD)

Procedure:

PRE-GROUP

E-mail the students' teachers the day before letting them know who you will be picking up and what time to expect you (about 5 minutes before the start of the lesson).

Remind the teachers and students during the morning announcements that you will be coming to their class a few minutes before it's time to go to lunch to retrieve students participating in *CCAL*.

Gather the students from their classrooms prior to lunch. The first few times may take longer as the students need to get used to the routine. This process will become easier, and students will only need to leave their classrooms a couple minutes early once the routine is established.

Have the students form a line in the hallway as you gather them from each classroom. Have your attendance chart handy to be sure you are gathering the correct students. Make sure the students have their lunches if they brought them from home (they often forget in the excitement). Remind the students of hallway behavior expectations as you head toward the lunchroom.

Walk the students into lunchroom and wait with them until the cafeteria personnel are ready to serve them. Don't expect personnel to serve the students early, but let them know you want the kids in the front of the line in order to have more time for the group. Kids with lunches from home can wait near the line.

Head to the location where *CCAL* is being held. Help the students find their assigned seats. As the weeks progress, students will automatically come to the *CCAL* area and know when to begin eating.

ROLL CALL

Each week will begin with attendance. Use the *Attendance Chart* (page 15 or CD).

Ask the students to show they are present by replying to the following *Camp Question of the Week*.

Would you prefer to stay overnight in a tent or in a cabin?

LESSON

Begin the lesson by saying:

Welcome to Camp Care-A-Lot. Some of you may be wondering why you are having lunch with the school counselor and what we will be doing in these sessions. We will be eating together for the next 10 weeks every (_DAY OF THE WEEK_) at (_TIME_). Sometimes, however, I may be asked to handle some important business. If that happens, I will let you know that our group meeting is canceled as soon as possible.

Some of you may have been hoping we were really going camping! You won't actually be leaving school, but you will be participating in fun activities with a camping theme. These activities will help you learn more about yourself and help you deal with difficult life situations.

You'll notice you have assigned seats. The area in which you are sitting is called your "cabin" and the people you are sitting with our called "campers." I hope that during our group you will learn from the other "campers" and help them as well. The students in your "cabin" are most likely all going through similar experiences in their lives. "Campers" in Camp Care-A-Lot might be experiencing the divorce or separation of their parents, a new stepparent and stepfamily, a death

in their family, or illness. Or they may need some encouragement with another difficult situation.

We are going to be discussing how to identify your feelings about what you are experiencing and how to get help when you need it. We will talk about feeling worried or angry, because many kids worry a lot or get angry when faced with a difficult situation. We will also be talking about bullying and teasing.

Each week we will discuss a different topic. And even though we will be talking about serious subjects, Camp Care-A-Lot will be fun, too.

The last week, we will have a wiener roast to celebrate all we have learned! Now, it isn't a real wiener roast. We won't have a fire, but I will cook hot dogs and serve chips and cookies.

REVIEW PROCEDURES

Tell the students:

Lunchroom supplies such as straws, napkins, and utensils are available.

Anytime someone feels uncomfortable sharing say, "Pass." This is called our Pass Rule.

What is said in Camp Care-A-Lot stays in Camp Care-A-Lot. For example, if I said that I sleep with my teddy bear, would I want that information to be shared on the playground? You may share things you learn from family members and other adults, but we do not share other students' names or situations. For example, you should not go home and say: "Guess what I found out today? I found out that there is kid in our group whose dad was arrested."

Treat everyone respectfully.

Any student keeping others from enjoying Camp Care-A-Lot may be asked to leave the group.

It is necessary that you finish your lunch before the end of the group session.

You need to clean up your "cabins" before you leave. Camp Care-A-Lot should be neat and clean.

FLASHLIGHT FEELINGS ACTIVITY (3-5 MINUTES)

This activity encourages the students to communicate their feelings and build trust and rapport with the "campers" in their "cabins." Students may find this exercise difficult for the first few weeks. However, the students will progress as they learn to trust and share.

Explain the following to the students:

Of all the things you will learn in CCAL in the next few weeks, I hope you will learn to be more comfortable talking with others about how you feel. It's hard even for adults to tell others how they are feeling. But talking about how you feel is important to your well-being. Each week, you will practice expressing your emotions by sharing how you feel this week or how your week is going.

Review how to play *Flashlight Feelings* (see page 13). Then have the students share how their week is going or how they are feeling with other members of their "cabin."

WHAT'S IN YOUR BACKPACK? ACTIVITY

Optional: Display the *What's In A Backpack.pdf* on an interactive whiteboard. Distribute a copy of *What's In Your Backpack?* and crayons to each student. Have the students draw the two items they would take in their backpack on the left side of the backpack, then color the right side of the backpack. Then ask the students to discuss with their "cabinmates" what two items they chose to bring to camp. If there is enough time, have some of the students share their ideas with the whole group. Some ideas could include pictures, favorite blanket or stuffed animal, journal, etc.

WHAT'S IN A BACKPACK?

What's In A Backpack.pdf

S'MORE ACTIVITIES

Depending on the amount of time left, choose one or more of the following activities.

Camp Ice Breaker

Tell the "campers" you are going to read some statements. If the statement applies to them, they should stand up. Tell the standing students to sit down, then read the next statement. Continue this process for each of the following statements:

1. Stand up if you have a brother.
2. Stand up if you are the youngest child in your family.
3. Stand up if you have a stepparent.
4. Stand up if you have a dog.
5. Stand up if you have step brothers or sisters.
6. Stand up if you are an only child.
7. Stand up if you have a sister.
8. Stand up if you have a new baby brother or sister in your home.

Camp Care-A-Lot Bingo (pages 22-29 or CD)

Bingo is a great time filler or ice breaker. There are six different bingo cards and calling cards. Reproduce the number needed for each student group making sure that each of the students in each of the "cabins" has a different bingo card. (Note: Each "cabin" should include a maximum of six students. When playing *Camp Care-A-Lot Bingo*, one student from each "cabin" could win at the same time.) Reproduce the calling cards, cut them out, and place them in a bag. Give each student markers (buttons, paperclips, etc.) for covering his/her card (five squares in a row, four corners, X, etc.). If you are allowing the students to take their cards home, make sure each student has a pencil to cross out the pictures on the card.

Camp Song: *I'm Going Wildlife Watching* (page 30 or CD)

Distribute a copy of *I'm Going Wildlife Watching* to each student. If you have an interactive whiteboard, you can display the Camp Song.pdf on the screen. Have the students sing the song with the leader.

What's In Your Backpack?

If you were heading to camp and could take only two extra things with you (other than your clothes and toiletries), what would you pack? **NO** electric or technological devices allowed!

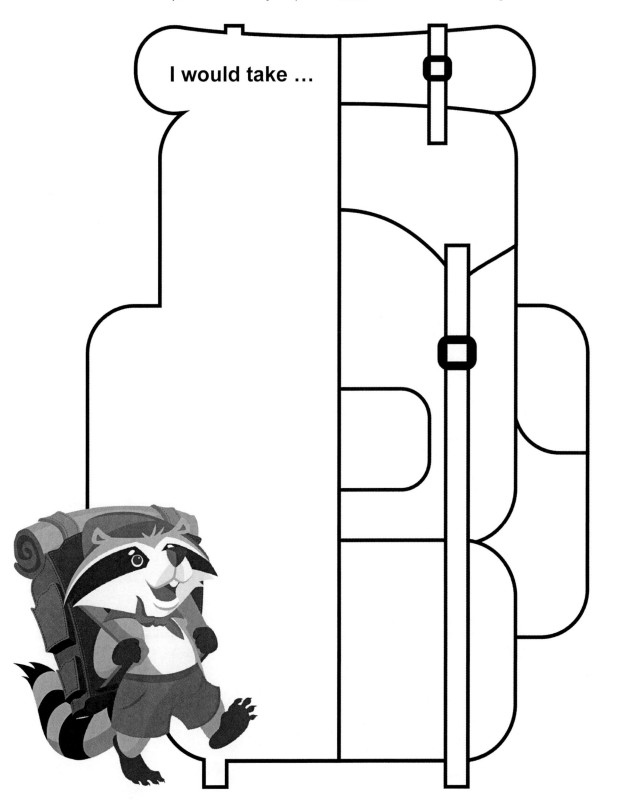

I would take …

CAMP CARE-A-LOT BINGO

CABIN

ME	Angry	Positive Thinking	Flashlight	Divorce
Family	Relaxing	Teasing	Reading Books	S'mores
Sad	Happy	Welcome to CCAL! FREE SPACE	Journal	Exercise
Fun!	Talking	Bully Buster BULLY FREE ZONE	Worried	Cabin
Friendship	Work Hard In School	Work Together	Moving	Lunch Time

CAMP CARE-A-LOT BINGO

C A B I N

Teasing	Fun!	S'mores	Cabin	Work Hard In School
Divorce	ME	Angry	Exercise	Flashlight
Relaxing	Family	Welcome to CCAL! FREE SPACE	Lunch Time	Work Together
Reading Books	Friendship	Journal	Sad	Moving
Worried	Positive Thinking	Talking	Bully Buster — BULLY FREE ZONE	Happy

Camp Care-A-Lot © 2016 Mar★co Products, Inc. 1-800-448-2197

CAMP CARE-A-LOT BINGO

CABIN

S'mores	Talking	Worried	Work Together	Family
Bully Buster — BULLY FREE ZONE	Fun!	ME	Friendship	Sad
Flashlight	Cabin	Welcome to CCAL! FREE SPACE	Positive Thinking	Moving
Lunch Time	Teasing	Divorce	Work Hard In School	Reading Books
Happy	Exercise	Angry	Journal	Relaxing

Camp Care-A-Lot © 2016 Mar★co Products, Inc. 1-800-448-2197

CAMP CARE-A-LOT BINGO

C	A	B	I	N
Reading Books	Exercise	Teasing	Lunch Time	Work Together
Work Hard In School	Angry	Moving	Fun!	Worried
Journal	Relaxing	Welcome to CCAL! FREE SPACE	Happy	Friendship
Family	Flashlight	Positive Thinking	S'mores	Divorce
Sad	Bully Buster BULLY FREE ZONE	Cabin	ME	Talking

CAMP CARE-A-LOT BINGO

CABIN

Work Hard In School	Cabin	Sad	ME	Exercise
Worried	Journal	Relaxing	Happy	Lunch Time
Divorce	Talking	Welcome to CCAL! FREE SPACE	Teasing	Reading Books
Angry	Moving	Family	Fun!	S'mores
Work Together	Bully Buster BULLY FREE ZONE	Friendship	Flashlight	Positive Thinking

Camp Care-A-Lot © 2016 Mar★co Products, Inc. 1-800-448-2197

CAMP CARE-A-LOT BINGO

C	A	B	I	N
C Journal	**A** Journal	**B** Journal	**I** Journal	**N** Journal
C Bully Buster	**A** Bully Buster	**B** Bully Buster	**I** Bully Buster	**N** Bully Buster
C Work Together	**A** Work Together	**B** Work Together	**I** Work Together	**N** Work Together
C Reading Books	**A** Reading Books	**B** Reading Books	**I** Reading Books	**N** Reading Books
C Moving	**A** Moving	**B** Moving	**I** Moving	**N** Moving
C Lunch Time	**A** Lunch Time	**B** Lunch Time	**I** Lunch Time	**N** Lunch Time
C Relaxing	**A** Relaxing	**B** Relaxing	**I** Relaxing	**N** Relaxing
C Worried	**A** Worried	**B** Worried	**I** Worried	**N** Worried
C Talking	**A** Talking	**B** Talking	**I** Talking	**N** Talking
C Sad	**A** Sad	**B** Sad	**I** Sad	**N** Sad
C Family	**A** Family	**B** Family	**I** Family	**N** Family
C Cabin	**A** Cabin	**B** Cabin	**I** Cabin	**N** Cabin

Camp Care-A-Lot © 2016 Mar★co Products, Inc. 1-800-448-2197

C	A	B	I	N
Work Hard In School	Work Hard In School	Work Hard In School	Work Hard In School	Work Hard In School
Teasing	Teasing	Teasing	Teasing	Teasing
Exercise	Exercise	Exercise	Exercise	Exercise
Friendship	Friendship	Friendship	Friendship	Friendship
Angry	Angry	Angry	Angry	Angry
Fun!	Fun!	Fun!	Fun!	Fun!
Flashlight	Flashlight	Flashlight	Flashlight	Flashlight
Divorce	Divorce	Divorce	Divorce	Divorce
Happy	Happy	Happy	Happy	Happy
Me	Me	Me	Me	Me
Positive Thinking	Positive Thinking	Positive Thinking	Positive Thinking	Positive Thinking
S'mores	S'mores	S'mores	S'mores	S'mores

I'm Going Wildlife Watching

Leader: We're going wildlife watching!
Students: We're going wildlife watching!

Leader: We're gonna see some big bears!
Students: We're gonna see some big bears!

Leader: I'm not afraid!
Students: I'm not afraid!

Leader: Are you?
Students: Are you?

Leader: Not me!
Students: Not me!

Leader: We're gonna go fishing.
Students: We're gonna go fishing.

Leader: Fishing for feelings.
Students: Fishing for feelings.

Leader: Sounds like fun.
Students: Sounds like fun.

Leader: Are you ready?
Students: Are you ready?

Leader: Yes I am!
Students: Yes I am!

Leader: We're gonna have some problems.
Students: We're gonna have some problems.

Leader: But that's OK.
Students: But that's OK.

Leader: We'll be ready for anything.
Students: We'll be ready for anything.

Leader: That comes our way.
Students: That comes our way.

Leader: I might be mad. (make an angry face)
Students: I might be mad. (make an angry face)

Leader: I might be sad. (make a sad face)
Students: I might be sad. (make a sad face)

Leader: I might be worried. (make a worried face)
Students: I might be worried. (make a worried face)

Leader: But that's OK.
Students: But that's OK.

Leader: Are you ready?
Students: Are you ready?

Leader: Yes I am!
Students: Yes I am!

GETTING TO KNOW ONESELF

Facilitator's Goal:

To have the students learn a little about themselves such as what they like and how they are different from others

Materials Needed:

For the facilitator:
- ☐ Table seat assignments
- ☐ Small flashlights for each student group/cabin
- ☐ *Attendance Chart* (page 15 or CD)
- ☐ Lunch supplies
- ☐ Trash can and cleaning supplies
- ☐ *Four Corners Sample* (optional, CD only)
- ☐ Interactive whiteboard (optional)

For each student:
- ☐ *Four Corners* (page 34 or CD)
- ☐ Crayons
- ☐ Pencil
- ☐ *Me* (optional activity, page 35 or CD)
- ☐ *Camp Activities* (optional activity, page 37 or CD)
- ☐ *Just Like Me, Not Like Me* (optional activity, page 38 or CD)

For each "cabin":
- ☐ *Jolly Campers* placed in a plastic sleeve (optional activity, page 36 or CD)
- ☐ Jolly Ranchers™ or another candy that have the five colors used on the *Jolly Camper* printout

Procedure:

ROLL CALL

Take attendance using the *Attendance Chart*. If some of the students have forgotten to come to *CCAL*, send a reliable student to the cafeteria to check in on them. If they choose not to come, make a note to talk with those students later.

Ask the students to show they are present by replying to the following *Camp Question of the Week*.

Would you prefer to tell or hear scary stories or silly stories around a camp fire?

REVIEW PROCEDURES

Tell the students:

Lunchroom supplies such as straws, napkins, and utensils are available.

Anytime someone feels uncomfortable sharing say, "Pass." This is called our Pass Rule.

What is said in **Camp Care-A-Lot** *stays in* **Camp Care-A-Lot.**

Treat everyone respectfully.

Any student keeping others from enjoying **Camp Care-A-Lot** *may be asked to leave the group.*

It is necessary that you finish your lunch before the end of the group session.

You need to clean up your "cabins" before you leave.

FLASHLIGHT FEELINGS ACTIVITY (3-5 MINUTES)

Briefly review how to play *Flashlight Feelings* (see page 13). Then have the students share how their week is going or how they are feeling with other members of their "cabin."

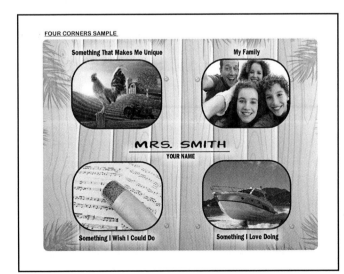

Four Corners Sample.pdf

FOUR CORNERS ACTIVITY

Optional: Display the *Four Corners Sample.pdf* on an interactive whiteboard. Distribute a copy of *Four Corners,* a pencil, and crayons to each student. Instruct the students to write their names in the middle of the page. Then, in each corner, have the students draw a picture or write about the following:

1. Something That Makes Me Unique
2. My Family
3. Something I Wish I Could Do
4. Something I Love Doing

S'MORE ACTIVITIES

Depending on the amount of time left, choose one or more of the following activities. The variety offers different activities for years to come. However, sometimes the kids enjoy doing the same activities year after year as well.

Me Activity (page 35 or CD)

This is a good activity to use with younger students or when little time is available. Have the students simply draw a picture of themselves. Then discuss how their pictures show how they are alike and different from others.

Jolly Campers Activity (page 36 or CD)

This activity can be used any week and is a great way for the "campers" in each "cabin" to get to know each other.

Instructions for the Jolly Campers activity:

1. Purchase Jolly Ranchers (original flavors) or another candy that has the five colors used on the *Jolly Camper* printout.

2. Prior to beginning the activity, place the *Jolly Campers* printouts in clear plastic sleeves and put one at each table along with one or two pieces of each color of candy. (*Note*: Both a color and grayscale version of the *Jolly Campers* printout is included on the CD. If you do not have access to color printing or you are using different colors of candy, print the grayscale version and color the candies the appropriate colors.)

3. Have the students choose a piece of candy. They must answer the question that corresponds with their chosen color. (*Note:* If the activity was used previously, tell the students they must choose a different color candy from the one chosen in the last activity.) At the end of the activity, the students may eat the candy (if allowed in your school's policy.)

Camp Activities (page 37 or CD)

Distribute a copy of *Camp Activities* and a pencil to each student. Then tell the students to look at the pictures on the activity sheet and circle those they would like to do.

Just Like Me, Not Like Me Activity (page 38 or CD)

Distribute a copy of *Just Like Me, Not Like Me* and a pencil to each student. Have the students roam around the room finding other students who are like them and who are *not* like them and write the names of the students in the spaces on their activity sheet.

My Family

Something I Love Doing

Something That Makes Me Unique

YOUR NAME

Something I Wish I Could Do

ME

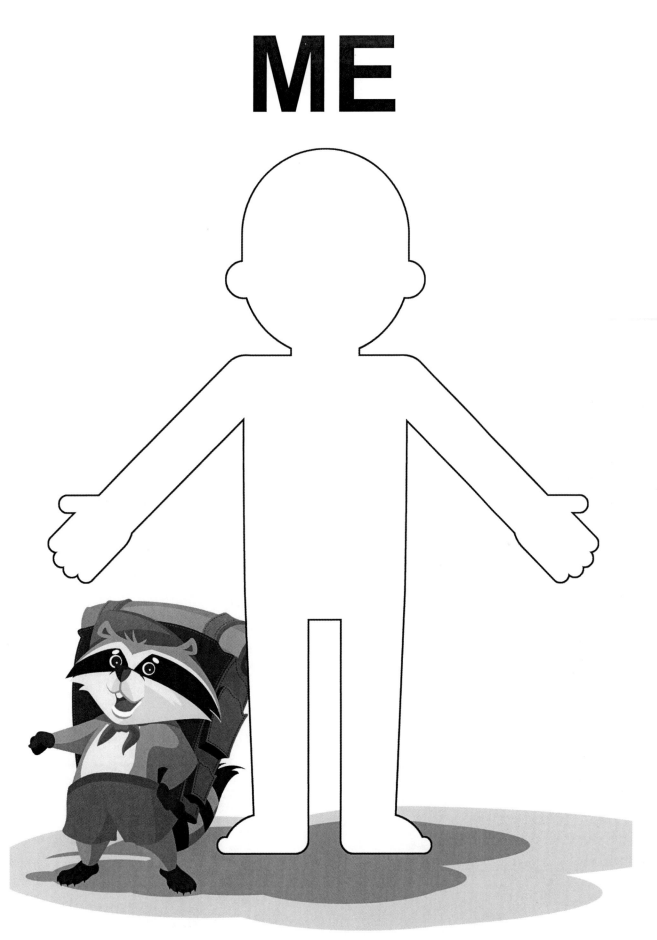

Jolly Campers

What is your favorite part of school?

What is your favorite place to eat?

What is your favorite TV show?

What is your favorite holiday?

What is your favorite food?

Camp Activities

What activities would you choose to do at camp? Circle as many as you would like.

Camp Care-A-Lot © 2016 Mar★co Products, Inc. 1-800-448-2197

JUST LIKE ME   NOT LIKE ME

Someone who has the same birth date as me.

Someone who has the same color of eyes as me.

Someone who has the same color of hair as me.

Someone who does NOT have the same birth date as me.

Someone who does NOT have the same color of eyes as me.

Someone who does NOT have the same color of hair as me.

My Family

Facilitator's Goals:

To have students learn who to consider "family"

To have students realize the importance of family celebrations and rituals

To have students recognize how their families are similar and different

To have students recognize ways in which their families have changed

Materials Needed:

For the facilitator:
- ☐ Table seat assignments
- ☐ Small flashlights for each student group/cabin
- ☐ *Attendance Chart* (page 15 or CD)
- ☐ Lunch supplies
- ☐ Trash can and cleaning supplies
- ☐ Interactive whiteboard or large piece of chart paper/dry erase board and markers (optional activity)

For each student:
- ☐ *My Family* (page 42 or CD)
- ☐ *My Family Has Changed* (page 43 or CD)
- ☐ Crayons
- ☐ Pencil

Procedure:

ROLL CALL

Take attendance using the *Attendance Chart*. If some of the students have forgotten to come to *CCAL*, send a reliable student to the cafeteria to check in on them. If they choose not to come, make a note to talk with those students later.

Ask the students to show they are present by replying to the following *Camp Question of the Week.*

Would you rather go camping with family or friends?

REVIEW PROCEDURES

Tell the students:

Lunchroom supplies such as straws, napkins, and utensils are available.

Anytime someone feels uncomfortable sharing say, "Pass." This is called our Pass Rule.

What is said in Camp Care-A-Lot *stays in* Camp Care-A-Lot.

Treat everyone respectfully.

Any student keeping others from enjoying Camp Care-A-Lot *may be asked to leave the group.*

It is necessary that you finish your lunch before the end of the group session.

You need to clean up your "cabins" before you leave.

FLASHLIGHT FEELINGS ACTIVITY (3-5 MINUTES)

If necessary, briefly review how to play *Flashlight Feelings* (see page 13). Then have the students share how their week is going or how they are feeling with other members of their "cabin."

MY FAMILY AND MY FAMILY HAS CHANGED ACTIVITY:

Distribute a copy of *My Family, My Family Has Changed,* crayons, and a pencil to each student. Have each student draw a picture of his/her family on the *My Family* activity sheet.

When the students have completed their drawings, have the "campers" in each "cabin" discuss how their families are different.

Then discuss the same topic with the entire group acknowledging different situations in the students' families such as stepparents, grandparents, foster parents, guardians, etc. Have the students share how their families celebrate birthdays, holidays, and family rituals such as mealtime and bedtime routines acknowledging different cultures, lifestyles, etc.

Discuss how families change (divorce, a move, a death, a sibling leaving for college, etc.). Have the students look at *My Family Has Changed* and instruct them to circle the situations their families have experienced.

S'MORE ACTIVITIES

Depending on the amount of time left, choose one or more of the following activities. The variety offers different activities for years to come. However, sometimes the kids enjoy doing the same activities year after year as well.

We Are Family Activity

Obtain several books which have pictures of families. If possible, play the song *We Are Family* by Sister Sledge (available on YouTube™). Play the song as the students are looking for pictures of families in the books. Then have the students discuss how the families found in the books are alike and different. Conclude the activity by having each "cabin" share with the entire group one way the pictures they found showed families were alike and one way the families were different.

Family Venn Diagram Activity

On an interactive whiteboard or large piece of chart paper/dry erase board, draw a Venn diagram. Compare and contrast two different families. Use imaginary families or ask for two volunteers to describe their families. "Campers" could also complete this activity with their "cabinmates" first, then share their findings with the entire group.

You Say It's Your Birthday Activity

Discuss how families celebrate birthdays and how their celebration rituals are similar and different. If possible, use props such as birthday hats and streamers.

My Family

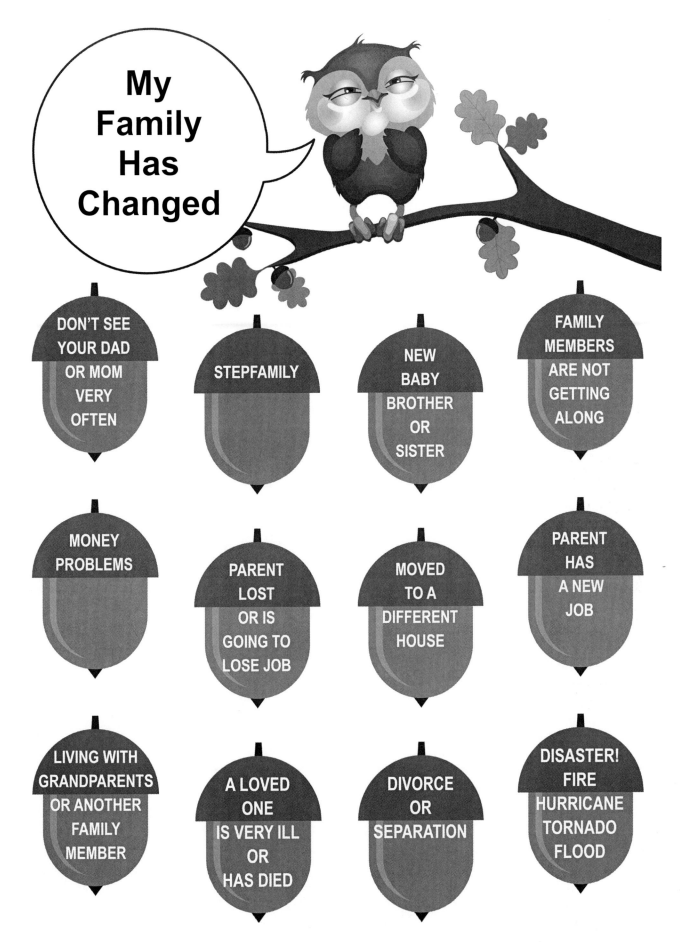

FISHING FOR FEELINGS

Facilitator's Goals:

To have students learn that experiencing different feelings is normal

To have students understand they may experience many feelings about the same situation

To help students identify how they are feeling and how to communicate with others

To help students communicate feelings verbally and nonverbally

Materials Needed:

For the facilitator:
- ☐ Table seat assignments
- ☐ Small flashlights for each student group/cabin
- ☐ *Attendance Chart* (page 15 or CD)
- ☐ Lunch supplies
- ☐ Trash can and cleaning supplies
- ☐ *I Say, You Say* (optional activity, page 52 or CD)
- ☐ Scissors

For each student:
- ☐ *Who Are Your Lifesavers?* (optional activity, page 51 or CD)
- ☐ Pencil

For each "cabin":
- ☐ *Let's Go Fishing For Feelings* (page 48 or CD)
- ☐ *It's In The Net* (optional activity, pages 49-50 or CD)
- ☐ Bowl or brown bag

Procedure:

ROLL CALL

Take attendance using the *Attendance Chart*. If some of the students have forgotten to come to *CCAL*, send a reliable student to the cafeteria to check in on them. If they choose not to come, make a note to talk with those students later.

Ask the students to show they are present by replying to the following *Camp Question of the Week.*

Would you prefer to go fishing or for a swim?

REVIEW PROCEDURES

Tell the students:

Lunchroom supplies such as straws, napkins, and utensils are available.

Anytime someone feels uncomfortable sharing say, "Pass." This is called our Pass Rule.

What is said in Camp Care-A-Lot *stays in* Camp Care-A-Lot.

Treat everyone respectfully.

Any student keeping others from enjoying Camp Care-A-Lot *may be asked to leave the group.*

It is necessary that you finish your lunch before the end of the group session.

You need to clean up your "cabins" before you leave.

FLASHLIGHT FEELINGS ACTIVITY (3-5 MINUTES)

If necessary, briefly review how to play *Flashlight Feelings* (see page 13). Then have the students share how their week is going or how they are feeling with other members of their "cabin."

DISCUSSION

In order to have the students better understand feelings, say the following:

Feelings are normal, and they are neither good nor bad. For example, feeling angry isn't pleasant, but anger can push people to change. Martin Luther King Jr. was angry at the way people were treated because of the color of their skin. He transformed his anger into action.

You can experience more than one feeling in a situation. How many of you have or are going to have a new baby sister or brother? How do you feel? (Some students may say they are excited and happy. Other students may say they are nervous, jealous, or worried.)

It is important to know how to communicate your feelings. Raise your hands if you have a dog or know someone who does. How do dogs show they are excited? (Wag their tails, jump up and down, lick you, etc.) *We don't wag our tails and lick each other when we are excited, but we do use nonverbal cues to show others how we feel. For example, if you saw me put my head down and cover my eyes you might think that I am feeling sad. If I am jumping up and down and throwing my arms up in the air you might think I am happy.*

Let's practice communicating our feelings by playing the Let's Go Fishing For Feelings Game.

LET'S GO FISHING FOR FEELINGS GAME

Make a copy of *Let's Go Fishing For Feelings* for each "cabin." Cut out the fish and put them in the bowl or brown bag. Give each group a bowl/bag. Then say:

Each of you will "go fishing." When you make your catch, read the feeling word printed on the fish, then tell your "cabinmates" about a time you felt that way.

Tell the students how much time they have to "fish." When the allotted time has elapsed, discuss each of the feelings—*Happy, Sad, Worried, Mad, Excited, Confused.* If any of the students did not have an opportunity to "go fishing," have them chose a feeling then tell the entire group about a time they experienced that feeling.

S'MORE ACTIVITIES

Depending on the amount of time left, choose one or more of the following activities. The variety offers different activities for years to come. However, sometimes the kids enjoy doing the same activities year after year as well.

How Do You Feel? Game

This game, which is similar to *Simon Says,* should be played with a large group of students. Introduce the activity by saying:

Sometimes we express our feelings without saying a word. This is called nonverbal communication. We are going to practice nonverbal communication by playing a game. I am going to name some situations, then you are going to express your feelings about these situations without saying a word. But before you show how you are feeling, you must say: "Simon didn't say!" Ready? Here we go. Don't forget to say: "Simon didn't say!"

Show me how you feel when:

1. *Your best friend asks you to go to the movies.*
2. *You earn an A+ on your spelling test.*
3. *When you wake up, it's raining. You are supposed to go swimming later and it's supposed to rain all day.*
4. *You find out your mom is having another baby.*
5. *People don't know how you are feeling.*

Optional: Have students name additional situations and continue playing the game.

It's In The Net Activity (pages 49-50 or CD)

Make a copy of *It's In The Net* for each "cabin." Cut out the fish and put them in the bowl or brown bag or, if you prefer, buy nets at a local Dollar Store. Give each "cabin" a bowl, bag, or net. Tell the "campers" to "go fishing." When a student makes a catch, he/she should read the statement printed on the fish, then tell his/her "cabinmates" how he/she would feel in that situation.

Who Are Your Lifesavers? Activity (page 51 or CD)

Distribute a copy of *Who Are Your Lifesavers?* and a pencil to each student. Tell the students to draw a line from the lifesaver to the boat if they could go to that person for help. Then have the students share the reasons for their choices.

I Say, You Say Activity (page 52 or CD)

This exercise focuses on empathy. Reproduce *I Say, You Say,* then cut the role-plays apart. Choose "campers" to role-play the parts, then have them read their parts aloud. The students may continue the role-play by adding their own actions and words. After each role-play, have the students explain how the role-play demonstrated empathic behavior.

Let's Go Fishing For Feelings

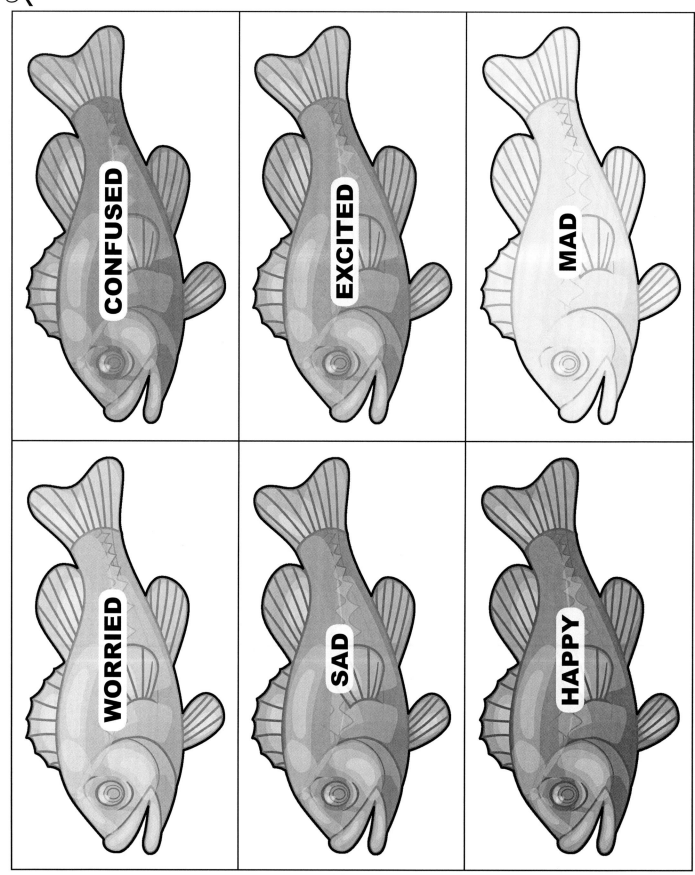

It's In The Net

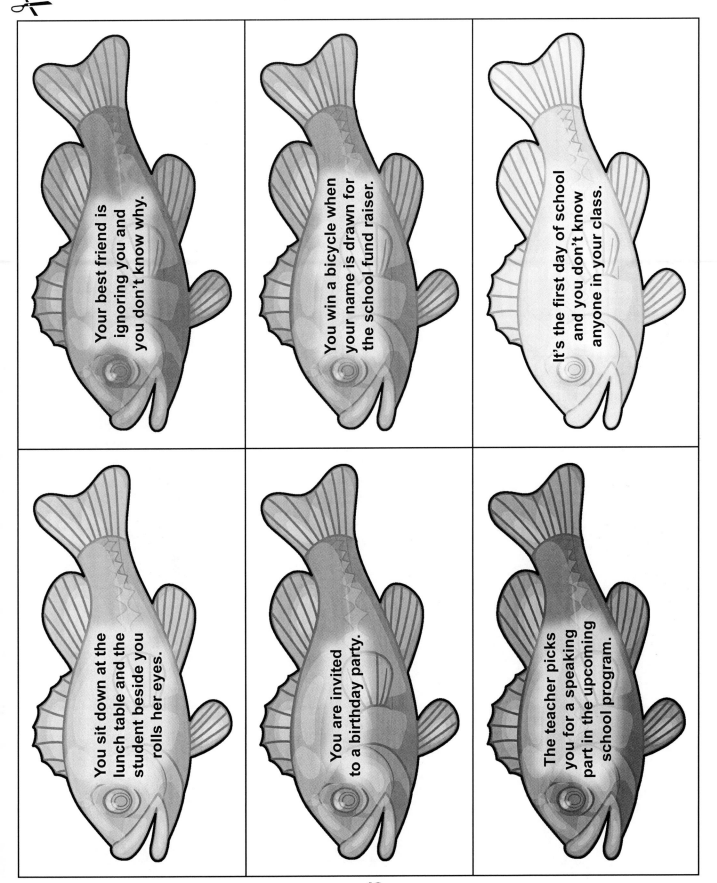

Your best friend is ignoring you and you don't know why.

You win a bicycle when your name is drawn for the school fund raiser.

It's the first day of school and you don't know anyone in your class.

You sit down at the lunch table and the student beside you rolls her eyes.

You are invited to a birthday party.

The teacher picks you for a speaking part in the upcoming school program.

It's In The Net

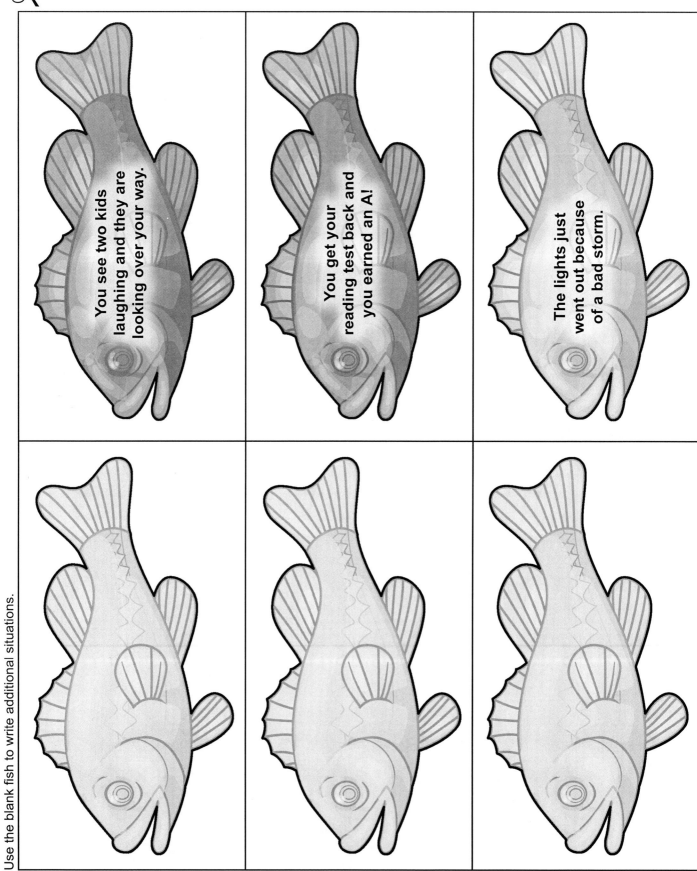

You see two kids laughing and they are looking over your way.

You get your reading test back and you earned an A!

The lights just went out because of a bad storm.

Use the blank fish to write additional situations.

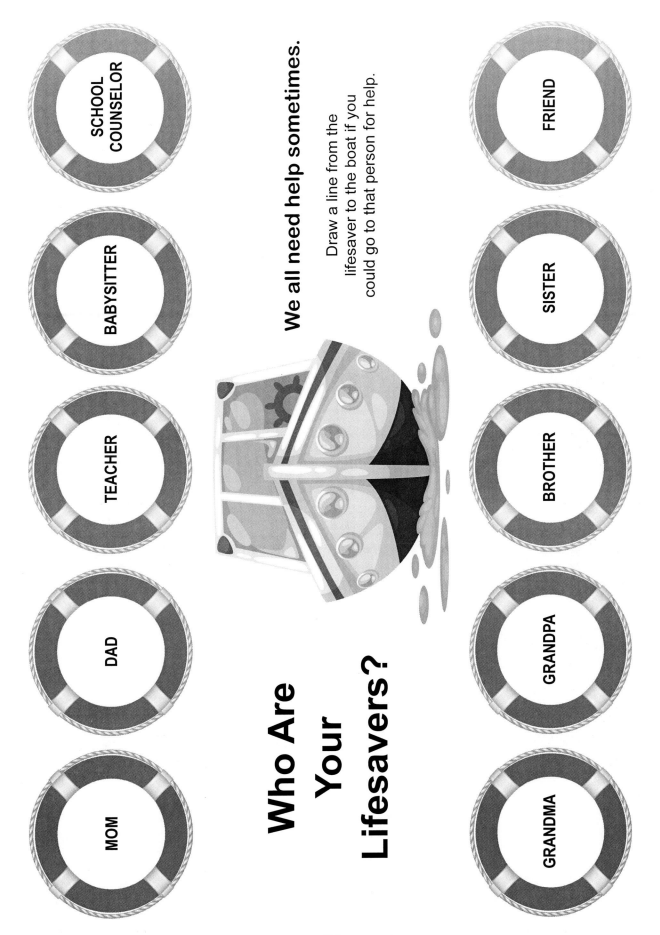

Who Are Your Lifesavers?

We all need help sometimes.

Draw a line from the lifesaver to the boat if you could go to that person for help.

SCHOOL COUNSELOR

BABYSITTER

TEACHER

DAD

MOM

FRIEND

SISTER

BROTHER

GRANDPA

GRANDMA

I Say, You Say

Camper 1: "I'm happy because I'm going to Florida on vacation."

Camper 2: "I hope you have fun."

Camper 1: "I'm sad because my Grandma is in the hospital."

Camper 2: "I hope she gets better."

Camper 1: "I'm worried because my parents are arguing."

Camper 2: "I don't like it when my parents argue, either."

Camper 1: "I'm mad because my mom won't let me go to the movies."

Camper 2: "I know how you feel, but maybe you can go next time."

Camper 1: "I'm scared to ride the bus because some kids are teasing me."

Camper 2: "It's horrible to feel that way. Have you told an adult?"

Camper 1: "I'm so excited. I won the classroom contest!"

Camper 2: "You must be so proud of yourself. Congratulations!"

TAKE A HIKE, WORRY

Facilitator's Goals:

To have the students understand what they can and cannot change

To help students understand that feeling worried is normal and worrying can have a positive aftereffect as long as it is controlled

Materials Needed:

For the facilitator:
- ☐ Table seat assignments
- ☐ Small flashlights for each student group/cabin
- ☐ *Attendance Chart* (page 15 or CD)
- ☐ Lunch supplies
- ☐ Trash can and cleaning supplies
- ☐ Interactive whiteboard or large piece of chart paper/dry erase board and markers
- ☐ Gather different sizes of rocks and write words associated with the word *worry* on them. Place the rocks in a container or bag. Or reproduce *Worries Weigh You Down* (page 58 or CD), cut out the paper rocks, and place them in a container or bag.
- ☐ Backpack

For each student:
- ☐ *Worry Action Plan* (page 57 or CD)
- ☐ *Worries Weigh You Down* (optional activity, page 58 or CD)
- ☐ *Take A Hike, Worry!* (optional activity, page 59 or CD)
- ☐ *My Worries* (optional activity, page 60 or CD)
- ☐ *Let Your Worries Go!* (optional activity, page 61 or CD)
- ☐ *Where Do You Feel Worry?* (optional activity, page 62 or CD)
- ☐ Pencil
- ☐ Crayons, including a yellow crayon (optional activities)

Procedure:

ROLL CALL

Take attendance using the *Attendance Chart*. If some of the students have forgotten to come to *CCAL*, send a reliable student to the cafeteria to check in on them. If they choose not to come, make a note to talk with those students later.

Ask the students to show they are present by replying to the following *Camp Question of the Week.*

> *Would you prefer to go on a hike or go on a bike ride?*

REVIEW PROCEDURES

Tell the students:

> *Lunchroom supplies such as straws, napkins, and utensils are available.*

> *Anytime someone feels uncomfortable sharing say, "Pass." This is called our Pass Rule.*

> *What is said in* **Camp Care-A-Lot** *stays in* **Camp Care-A-Lot.**

> *Treat everyone respectfully.*

> *Any student keeping others from enjoying* **Camp Care-A-Lot** *may be asked to leave the group.*

> *It is necessary that you finish your lunch before the end of the group session.*

> *You need to clean up your "cabins" before you leave.*

FLASHLIGHT FEELINGS ACTIVITY (3-5 MINUTES)

If necessary, briefly review how to play *Flashlight Feelings* (see page 13). Then have the students share how their week is going or how they are feeling with other members of their "cabin."

ACTIVITY

Introduce the activity by saying:

> *Has anyone ever been on a hike? Anytime you take a long walk or hike it isn't easy if you have to carry a lot. Even if you use a backpack to help carry everything you need, it can be difficult. That backpack can get heavy! When you worry, you might experience a similar feeling. Carrying all your worries with you can weigh you down and tire you out.*

Conduct a backpack demonstration. One at a time, take the actual or paper rocks from the bag/container and put them in the backpack. Emphasize how with each rock the backpack gets heavier to lift and carry.

If time allows, have the "campers" in each "cabin" discuss what students their age worry about.

Use any or all of the following information to teach and discuss dealing with anxiety and worrying.

1. Ask the following questions:

   Who do you know that worries and how do you know that they are worried? What are some signs that a person may be worrying too much? (If not mentioned, include the following answers: stomach hurts, headaches, not sleeping or sleeping too much, not eating or eating too much, avoiding doing things like coming to school or going to a friend's house, etc.)

   How do you react when you are worried? (Have the students share how they react or feel when they are worried. For example: "I always know I am worried about something if my stomach hurts.")

2. Discuss strategies to reduce worry:

   Make a worry list.

   Decide what you need to change and make a plan to change.

   Let go of the worries you can't change.

   Be active. Exercise and release built up anxiety.

   Relax. Breathe deeply and think about a calming place like a beach or park.

   Talk with someone.

3. Discuss how worry can be helpful in motivating people to get things done. Say:

   Sometimes it is OK to worry. What would happen if your parents didn't worry at all about getting the bills paid, getting you to school, or feeding you? What would happen if you didn't worry about your grades or how you treated your friends?

Have all the "campers" share what kids their age worry about. Write their ideas on the Interactive whiteboard or large piece of chart paper/dry erase board. Below is a list of some things third graders worry about:

Friends	Parents
Something bad happening to them	Statewide testing
Grades	Storms
Fire	Floods

Camp Care-A-Lot © 2016 Mar★co Products, Inc. 1-800-448-2197

Review each mentioned worry, then discuss whether or not they would have control over that worry. For example, you might say:

> ***Some of you mentioned you are afraid of storms. Can we control Mother Nature?*** (No.) ***What can we do when we know there is potential for a bad storm?*** (Review where the safe spot is in your house; make sure you are prepared with water, flashlights, blankets, etc.; watch the weather forecast to track the storm.)

Distribute a copy of the *Worry Action Plan* and a pencil to each student. Have the students complete the activity sheet. Then allow those "campers" who wish to do so to share their ideas with either the entire group or their "cabinmates."

S'MORE ACTIVITIES

Depending on the amount of time left, choose one or more of the following activities. The variety offers different activities for years to come.

Worries Weigh You Down Activity (page 58 or CD)

Distribute a copy of *Worries Weigh You Down,* crayons, and a pencil to each student. Have the students look at the worries printed on the stones, then lightly color those that apply to them. Other worries students experience can be written on the blank stones. Discuss the completed activity sheets.

Take A Hike, Worry Activity (page 59 or CD)

Distribute a copy of *Take A Hike, Worry* and a pencil to each student. Then have the students write a worry they have experienced in each bootprint. Have those students who wish to do so share what they wrote with the entire group or their "cabinmates."

My Worries Activity (page 60 or CD)

Distribute a copy of *My Worries* and a yellow crayon to each student. Have the students look at the worries printed on the activity sheet, then lightly color the honeycomb if they are currently experiencing that worry. Have those students who wish to do so share what they are worrying about with the entire group or their "cabinmates."

Let Your Worries Go! Activity (page 61 or CD)

Distribute a copy of *Let Your Worries Go!* and a pencil to each student. Have the students complete the handout by writing a worry they cannot change in each balloon. Have those students who wish to do so share what they have written with the entire group or their "cabinmates."

Where Do You Feel Worry? Activity (page 62 or CD)

Distribute a copy of *Where Do You Feel Worry?*, crayons, and a pencil to each student. Have the students write on the handout where they feel stress and worry.

WORRY
Action Plan

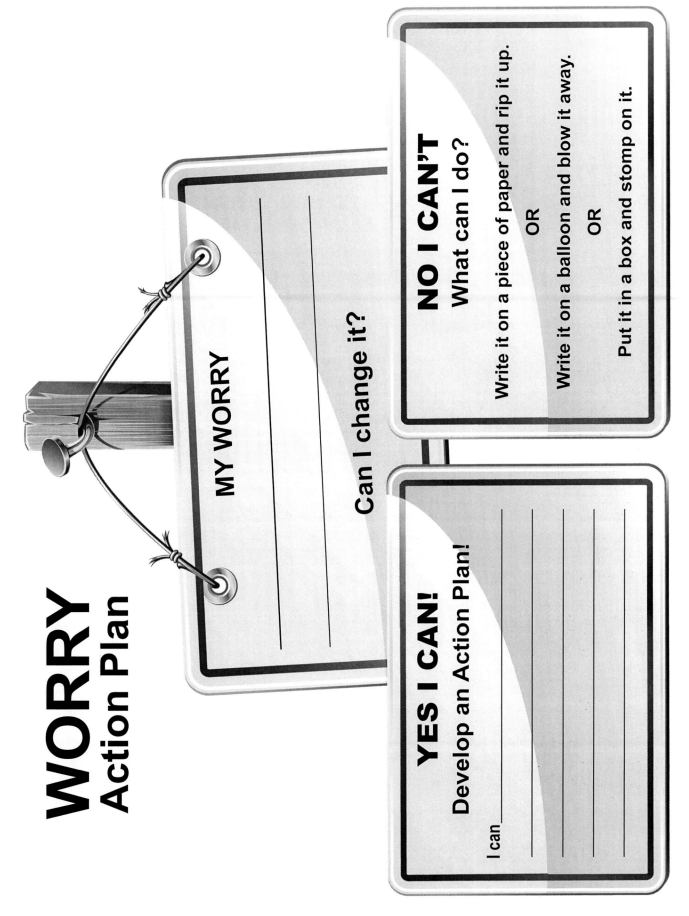

MY WORRY

Can I change it?

NO I CAN'T

What can I do?

Write it on a piece of paper and rip it up.

OR

Write it on a balloon and blow it away.

OR

Put it in a box and stomp on it.

YES I CAN!

Develop an Action Plan!

I can

Camp Care-A-Lot © 2016 Mar★co Products, Inc. 1-800-448-2197

Worries Weigh You Down

Color the worries that might weigh you down.
Write any other worries you have on the empty rocks.

DAD

SPORTS

MOM

BROTHER

GRADES

SISTER

TESTS

FRIENDS

THE WAY I LOOK

STORMS

Camp Care-A-Lot © 2016 Mar★co Products, Inc. 1-800-448-2197

Take A Hike, Worry

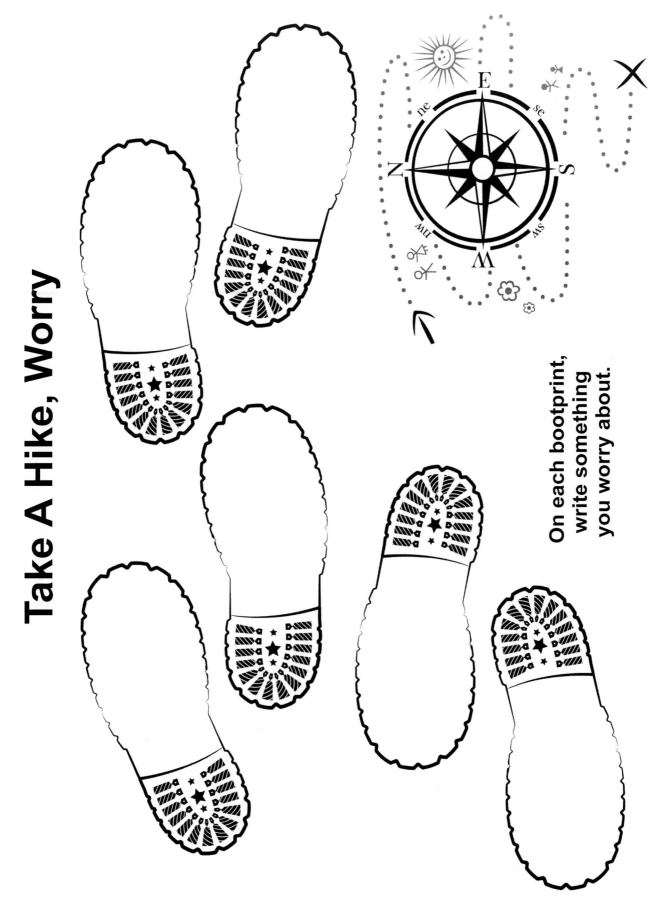

On each bootprint, write something you worry about.

Camp Care-A-Lot © 2016 Mar★co Products, Inc. 1-800-448-2197

My Worries

For each thing you are worrying about, color the honeycomb yellow.

MOM

DAD

PETS

TESTS

FRIENDS

STORMS

ILLNESS

MATH

STRANGERS

BULLYING

HOMEWORK

GRADES

HOW I LOOK

FAMILY

BEING HOME ALONE

MONEY

DEATH

Let Your Worries Go!

**Write the worries you
cannot change in each balloon.**

Where Do You Feel Worry?

When you are worried, do you feel well?
Does your stomach hurt or do you get a headache?

Draw an X or color the areas of the body where you feel worry.

ANGER-MANAGEMENT

Facilitator's Goals:

To have students understand that anger is normal

To have students recognize that the way they deal with anger can have positive or negative consequences

To teach students ways to cope when they are angry

Materials Needed:

For the facilitator:
- ☐ Table seat assignments
- ☐ Small flashlights for each student group/cabin
- ☐ *Attendance Chart* (page 15 or CD)
- ☐ Lunch supplies
- ☐ Trash can and cleaning supplies
- ☐ *What Works For You?* (optional activity, page 67 or CD)
- ☐ *Who's In Control?* (optional activity, page 68 or CD)
- ☐ Balloon (*The Balloon Demonstration*–optional activity, pages 69-70 or CD)
- ☐ Box of cereal (*The Balloon Demonstration*–optional activity, pages 69-70 or CD)
- ☐ Desk or table (*The Balloon Demonstration*–optional activity, pages 69-70 or CD)

For each student:
- ☐ Paper
- ☐ Pencil

Procedure:

ROLL CALL

Take attendance using the *Attendance Chart*. If some of the students have forgotten to come to *CCAL*, send a reliable student to the cafeteria to check in on them. If they choose not to come, make a note to talk with those students later.

Ask the students to show they are present by replying to the following *Camp Question of the Week.*

Would you prefer to climb a tree or relax under a tree?

REVIEW PROCEDURES

Tell the students:

Lunchroom supplies such as straws, napkins, and utensils are available.

Anytime someone feels uncomfortable sharing say, "Pass." This is called our Pass Rule.

What is said in Camp Care-A-Lot *stays in* Camp Care-A-Lot.

Treat everyone respectfully.

Any student keeping others from enjoying Camp Care-A-Lot *may be asked to leave the group.*

It is necessary that you finish your lunch before the end of the group session.

You need to clean up your "cabins" before you leave.

FLASHLIGHT FEELINGS ACTIVITY (3-5 MINUTES)

If necessary, briefly review how to play *Flashlight Feelings* (see page 13). Then have the students share how their week is going or how they are feeling with other members of their "cabin."

DISCUSSION

Use any or all of the following information to teach and discuss dealing with anger. Say:

Anger is neither good nor bad. It's how you cope with your anger that can be beneficial or harmful.

Everyone gets angry at times. For example, you might get angry when you don't find what you want at the store, a friend won't play with you or has betrayed you, at how someone is being treated, or that you can't go swimming because it's raining.

Remember, being angry isn't pleasant, but anger can push people to change. Martin Luther King Jr. was angry at the way people were treated because of the color of their skin. He transformed his anger into action and chose not to be violent but to use his words to express his anger.

Then ask:

How do you express your anger?

Is the way you express your anger helpful or harmful to yourself or others?

ANGER EQUATION ACTIVITY

Introduce the activity by saying:

Imagine the following situation is about you. Listen and think about how you would feel.

It's morning. You wake up late and your alarm is blaring. Your mom walks into your bedroom and yells, "You are late!" You can't find one of your shoes. At breakfast, you find your little sister has eaten all of your favorite cereal. Then your brother walks by and hits you in the hallway, and your mom yells at you when you scream back at him. Now the bus is coming, and you don't have your backpack ready. When you get on the bus, no one will let you sit with them. You walk into your classroom and realize you forgot your homework folder on the kitchen table. You get to your seat and your neighbor has all of her things touching your desk. And the day goes on ...

Distribute a piece of paper and a pencil to each student. Then ask the students to come up with a number that would represent the average number of times they could become angry in a day. After the students have selected their numbers, continue the activity by saying:

Throughout the day, you might be faced with "triggers" that aggravate you and people who "push your buttons." How many times do you think an average _____ grader could potentially get angry in one day? (Wait for a few students to answer.)

How many anger triggers are there in your day? (Wait for a few students to answer, noting if the numbers are average or large.)

On a terrible day, how many times do you actually lose your temper, throw a fit, or have an outburst? (Wait for the students' answers, noting if any students respond with 20 or above which is a large number.)

Now, we are going to do some math. On your piece of paper, write the number of times you may be triggered in a day, minus the number of times you actually lose your temper or blow up.

Have the students tell their answers. Then say:

> *Your answer is the number of times you controlled your anger. What helped you control your anger?*
>
> *Remember, you can control your anger better if you do not lose control.*

S'MORE ACTIVITIES

Depending on the amount of time left, choose one or more of the following activities. The variety offers different activities for years to come.

***What Works For You?* Activity** (page 67 or CD)

Read the information, then discuss the anger-management strategies with the entire group.

***Who's In Control?* Activity** (page 68 or CD)

Present the activity to help students learn about self control and how to stay in control when faced with a difficult situation.

The Balloon Demonstration (pages 69-70 or CD)

Use a balloon to demonstrate how to can gain self control. Obtain a balloon and a box of cereal before beginning the activity. Have a desk or table available.

What Works For You?

Introduce the activity by saying:

When you get angry, you might do something you later regret like screaming at your mom or ripping up your social studies report. But you don't always have to lose control. You can control your anger.

First, it is important to know that when you are angry your body changes. Everyone show me what you look like when you feel angry.

Wait for the students to make angry expressions. Then say:

When you feel angry your body becomes tense. You might clench your hands and before long you are breathing fast and feel hot. Your heart might feel like it could beat out of your chest and you could pop! When this happens, you aren't thinking clearly and you let your anger get the best of you. This is when you might make choices that you later regret. This is when you have to stop, allow your body to calm down, and take a deep breath to relax.

Let's talk about some other techniques you could use to calm down.

Ask the students to share some other ways they could calm down. Their responses might include:

- Think of something you are looking forward to or a place where you are happy (swimming in the summer, relaxing on a beach, taking a walk in a park, etc.)

- Exercise

- Write a letter or in your journal

- Draw a picture

- Talk with someone you trust

- Do something else you enjoy for awhile so you have a fresh perspective (play a computer game, watch TV, work on a puzzle, etc.)

- Sleep

- Cry

- Read

Who's In Control?

Obtain a remote control. Then, following the instructions below, present the activity.

1. Take a remote control and wave it at the students as you press the buttons.

2. Act frustrated because the remote control is not "working" on them.

3. Pretend you don't understand why it isn't working. Hit and shake the remote control as if you are trying to get the batteries to work.

4. Tell the students: "I don't know why this remote control isn't working."

5. The students should then begin to yell out: "It doesn't work on people!"

6. Hold a short discussion on self control and the fact that people are not controlled by other people.

7. Ask the students: "Who's in control of a person?" (himself/herself)

8. Discuss how students often say: "He made me do it!" Then ask: "Did someone make you kick the door? Did someone make you hit your sister?"

9. Say: "When someone pushes your 'buttons,' it is your choice to respond by kicking, hitting or shouting."

10. Then say: "You must learn to recognize when you are getting your 'buttons' pushed and how to resist losing your self control."

YOU ARE IN CONTROL!

The Balloon Demonstration

Put the balloon and box of cereal on a desk or table. Then, say:

When you are angry, you may feel like you could pop. People don't really pop, but they can lose control. I'm going to show you how people lose control, then demonstrate how you can keep yourselves from losing control.

Present the first demonstration.

DEMONSTRATION 1

10 year old Abigail doesn't like to wake up. Her mom is repeatedly yelling at her to get out of bed. Abigail says:

"UGH! I'm so mad!" (Blow some air into the balloon to show how Abigail feels.)

Abigail starts to get dressed and realizes she can't find matching socks. She clenches her fists and says:

"UGH! I'm so mad!" (Blow more air into the balloon.)

As Abigail walks down the hall, her sister bumps into her. Abigail stomps her foot and says:

"I'm **sooooo** mad!" (Blow more air into the balloon.)

Next, Abigail goes into the kitchen and realizes that her sister ate all of her favorite breakfast cereal and she doesn't have anything to eat that she likes. She says:

"I'm **sooooo sooooo** mad!" (Blow more air into the balloon until it is full.)

By this time, Abigail is so angry that she feels like she could pop. (Show how the balloon is full of air.) But Abigail doesn't pop, she … **LOSES CONTROL!** (Release the balloon so it flies through the air.) Abigail screams at her sister and tosses the empty box of cereal off the counter. (Toss the box of cereal on the floor.) Just then, Abigail's mom walks into the kitchen. She asks Abigail to explain her actions and says she is grounded for one night.

Put the balloon on the desk or table and the box of cereal on a nearby desk or table. Present the second demonstration.

DEMONSTRATION #2

10 year old Abigail doesn't like to wake up. Her mom is repeatedly yelling at her to get out of bed. Abigail says:

"UGH! I'm so mad!" (Blow some air into the balloon to show how Abigail feels.) "But I'm not going to ruin my day. I have fun things planned today." (Release some air out of the balloon.)

Abigail starts to get dressed and realizes she can't find matching socks. She clenches her fists and says to herself:

"UGH! I'm so mad!" (Blow more air into the balloon.)

Abigail takes a moment to think, then says:

"I think I saw some clean clothes in the laundry room." (Release some air out of the balloon.)

As Abigail walks down the hall, her sister bumps into her. Abigail stomps her foot and says:

"I'm **sooooo** mad!" (Blow more air into the balloon.)

Abigail takes a deep breath and tells herself:

"I'm not going to let her push my buttons." (Release some air out of the balloon.)

Next, Abigail goes into the kitchen and realizes that her sister ate all of her favorite breakfast cereal and she doesn't have anything to eat that she likes. She says:

"I'm **sooooo sooooo** mad!" (Blow more air into the balloon.)

Just then, Abigail's mom walks into the kitchen. Abigail tells her mom she's having a rough day. Her mom reminds her that there is extra cereal in the pantry. (Point to the box of cereal.) She smiles at her mom and says:

"Thank you." (Release all the air from the balloon.)

This time, "campers," the story had a much happier ending. Abigail calmed down and she **DIDN'T** lose control!

BULLYING AND TEASING

Facilitator's Goals:

To teach students to be confident when faced with teasing or bullying situations

To help students understand the difference between teasing and bullying

To help students recognize how their own behavior might be affecting others

Materials Needed:

For the facilitator:
- ☐ Table seat assignments
- ☐ Small flashlights for each student group/cabin
- ☐ *Attendance Chart* (page 15 or CD)
- ☐ Lunch supplies
- ☐ Trash can and cleaning supplies
- ☐ Interactive whiteboard or large piece of chart paper/dry erase board and markers
- ☐ Ball or stress ball

For each student: None

Procedure:

ROLL CALL

Take attendance using the *Attendance Chart*. If some of the students have forgotten to come to *CCAL*, send a reliable student to the cafeteria to check in on them. If they choose not to come, make a note to talk with those students later.

Ask the students to show they are present by replying to the following *Camp Question of the Week.*

Would you prefer to read a book or be an actor in a play?

REVIEW PROCEDURES

Tell the students:

> *Lunchroom supplies such as straws, napkins, and utensils are available.*
>
> *Anytime someone feels uncomfortable sharing say, "Pass." This is called our Pass Rule.*
>
> *What is said in Camp Care-A-Lot stays in Camp Care-A-Lot.*
>
> *Treat everyone respectfully.*
>
> *Any student keeping others from enjoying Camp Care-A-Lot may be asked to leave the group.*
>
> *It is necessary that you finish your lunch before the end of the group session.*
>
> *You need to clean up your "cabins" before you leave.*

FLASHLIGHT FEELINGS ACTIVITY (3-5 MINUTES)

If necessary, briefly review how to play *Flashlight Feelings* (see page 13). Then have the students share how their week is going or how they are feeling with other members of their "cabin."

KEEP YOUR POWER ACTIVITY

Have a ball or stress ball available. Begin the activity by saying:

> *We all know someone who has been teased or bullied or maybe you have been teased or bullied. How does someone feel when they are teased or bullied?*

Write the students' suggested feelings on the board/chart paper. If not mentioned, include *lonely, angry, sad, frustrated*, and *powerless*. After writing each feeling on the board/chart paper, circle or underline the word if feeling that way could have negative or hurtful ramifications.

Hold up the ball, then ask a student to try to pull it of your hand. Holding tightly onto the ball, continue the activity by saying:

> *On a good day, when everything is going well, you feel in control and powerful. You are full of positive energy.*

Then someone comes along and criticizes you. Perhaps this person makes fun of your shoes or your hair. All of a sudden, your positive energy decreases and you don't feel as powerful. You begin to question how you look.

Have the student to try to pull the ball out of your hand again, then have the student return to his/her seat. Say:

Imagine someone is attempting to take some of your power away. It is your job to figure out how to keep your power and not let what others say or do take it away. In order to do this, here are some ideas that can be helpful.

First, let's talk about <u>BODY LANGUAGE</u>. Body language is an important part of the way we communicate. We can show others how we feel without saying a word. In fact, 85% of our communication with others is nonverbal. Body language includes:

- *Eye contact: Are you looking directly at someone or avoiding eye contact?*
- *Facial expressions: You can often tell if a person is angry, sad, or happy by the expression on his or her face.*
- *Posture: Standing straight might mean you feel confident. Slouching might mean you feel scared or nervous.*
- *Gestures: People often use their hands and arms to emphasize what they are saying* (clapping, giving a "thumbs up.")

Next, let's talk about <u>IGNORING</u> someone who is trying to take your power away. Students often tell me they have tried to ignore someone who is criticizing or bothering them. But I have found that students are "ignoring" all wrong. I will tell you about two different situations and you will tell me which one offers a better way to react. I need one assistant to serve as the person attempting to take away my power.

Select a student to help you demonstrate the situations by playing the part of Morgan. Tell that student to continually tap on your shoulder. Then present Scene 1 with eyes downcast, shoulders hunched, and looking defeated.

<u>SCENE 1</u>

In a whining voice, say to the entire group:

Morgan won't stop bothering me! He's/She's always picking on me. I've been ignoring him/her but it's not working. I don't know what to do!

Then ask the students:

Who has the power in this situation? (Morgan has the power.)

Camp Care-A-Lot © 2016 Mar★co Products, Inc. 1-800-448-2197

<u>SCENE 2</u> (Continue to ignore the student tapping on your shoulder. Stand up straight, shoulders back, and looking confident.)

In a strong confident voice, ask the entire group:

> **Is there anything fun happening in school this week?** or **Did you have a good weekend?**

Then ask the students:

> **Who has the power in this situation?** (You have the power.)

Have the student playing Morgan return to his/her seat, then continue the activity by saying:

> **My body language in each scene was different. Even though I am not talking to Morgan in the first scene, my body language clearly showed that I felt defeated. Morgan had my power! In the second scene, I am showing no signs at all that Morgan is bothering me. I knew the whole time Morgan was tapping on my shoulder, but I didn't let him/her know I was paying attention. I ignored Morgan.**

Present the next technique by saying:

> **The next way to keep your power is to <u>STAND UP FOR YOURSELF</u>. To do this, you have to speak with confidence and say it like you mean it. I'm going to enact two more situations. Tell me which one is more convincing.**

Looking defeated, say in a whining voice:

> **Stop! Leave me alone.**

Then using a strong voice with confident body language, say:

> **Stop! Leave me alone.**

Ask the students:

> **In the two scenes, I used the exact same words. Was the first statement convincing?** (No, because I appeared to be powerless.)

> **Was the second statement convincing?** (Yes, because I sent the message that I meant business.)

Present the next technique by saying:

> **Another way to keep your power is to have a <u>SENSE OF HUMOR</u>. Let's say someone says to me: "Ewww ... your shirt is dirty. That's nasty!"**

I could respond by saying:

Thanks for noticing. That's my dirt collection. I've been working on it for several days now!

STAND UP FOR OTHERS ACTIVITY

Introduce the topic by saying:

You have learned several ways to keep your power and stand up for yourself. Now we will talk about how you can stand up for others. One way to stop bullying and teasing is to be aware of situations where you can make a difference. There may be times when you didn't realize you were actually helping a bully. Let me show you what I'm talking about. I'll need another helper.

Choose a student who is resilient and will be a good sport to play the part of The Bully. Without the rest of the group hearing, explain to the student that when he/she comes back into the room he/she should look at you and say aloud: "Your hair looks funny. What did you do, stick your finger in a light socket?" Have the student leave the room.

Then, tell the group:

When <u>NAME OF STUDENT</u> comes back into the room, he/she will say something. When you hear it, everyone is to laugh with him/her.

When the student returns to the room and says his/her lines, the rest of the class should laugh. Show you are feeling sad and powerless by putting your head down and acting like you want to turn around and hide. Then make a tiny gesture with your fingers and say:

I feel this big. I just want to hide. In fact, I am probably going to tell the teacher that my stomach hurts and I need to go see the nurse. I won't want to come back tomorrow either because I'm terrified of what you will all think of me.

Say to the students:

Point to the student who is playing The Bully and demonstrate with your fingers, with five being the most and one being the least, how powerful he/she feels. (pause)*You are right, The Bully feels very powerful because he/she got everyone to laugh at me. In fact, The Bully feels like he/she is quite the comedian. The Bully likes the attention and wants to get more of it. So what do you think The Bully will do next?*

Wait for the students' answers. Then say:

The Bully will try to gain more power by doing it again. Only this time, it might be you that he/she makes a joke about. It might be you that everyone is laughing at, and it won't be funny to you. Let's rewind this situation and see how it can end differently. This time, when our actor says his/her lines, I don't want anyone to laugh. Instead, I need a couple of you to stick up for me by saying something like, "Don't listen to The Bully, your hair looks fine."

Repeat the skit using the same words as before. When the skit is completed, say to the students:

This time I feel much better. I still feel powerful. Having people stick up for me made all the difference.

Then ask the students:

How do you feel when you speak up and stick up for someone? (The students will reply they feel good.)

How would The Bully feel? (Not feeling powerful at all.)

Will The Bully be likely to say something mean to someone else? (Probably not, because he/she did not receive the same feedback as before. The Bully was put in his/her place and has lost his/her power.)

Conclude the activity by saying:

We all can make a difference by standing up for others. If you are in a situation where you see someone being bullied or teased, try to help.

If you are worried about getting into a harmful situation, ask an adult for help.

Remember and practice all the strategies we have talked about today.

REFRAMING THINKING

Facilitator's Goal:

To teach students how to change negative thinking into positive thinking

Materials Needed:

For the facilitator:
- ☐ Table seat assignments
- ☐ Small flashlights for each student group/cabin
- ☐ *Attendance Chart* (page 15 or CD)
- ☐ Lunch supplies
- ☐ Trash can and cleaning supplies

For each student: None

For each K-Grade 2 "cabin":
- ☐ *Thought Bubble* (page 82 or CD) laminated and attached to a stick or a ruler to make a *Thinking Stick*

For each Grade 3-5 "cabin":
- ☐ *Thinking Situations* (page 80 or CD)
- ☐ *What Is Another Way Of Looking At The Situation?* (page 81 or CD)
- ☐ Paper
- ☐ Pencils

Procedure:

ROLL CALL

Take attendance using the *Attendance Chart*. If some of the students have forgotten to come to *CCAL*, send a reliable student to the cafeteria to check in on them. If they choose not to come, make a note to talk with those students later.

Ask the students to show they are present by replying to the following *Camp Question of the Week*.

Would you prefer to plant flowers or paint a picture of flowers?

REVIEW PROCEDURES

Tell the students:

> *Lunchroom supplies such as straws, napkins, and utensils are available.*

> *Anytime someone feels uncomfortable sharing say, "Pass." This is called our Pass Rule.*

> *What is said in Camp Care-A-Lot stays in Camp Care-A-Lot.*

> *Treat everyone respectfully.*

> *Any student keeping others from enjoying Camp Care-A-Lot may be asked to leave the group.*

> *It is necessary that you finish your lunch before the end of the group session.*

> *You need to clean up your "cabins" before you leave.*

FLASHLIGHT FEELINGS ACTIVITY (3-5 MINUTES)

If necessary, briefly review how to play *Flashlight Feelings* (see page 13). Then have the students share how their week is going or how they are feeling with other members of their "cabin."

ACTIVITY

This lesson offers two activities: *Thinking Situations* is for students in Grades 3-5 and the *Thought Bubble* works best with students in Grades K-2.

Introduce the activity by saying:

> *Today we are going to discuss how your thinking affects your success. For example, if you believe you will miss the ball in a kick ball game, you probably will. Listen as these three ways of thinking are explained, then each of you can reflect on which type or types of thinker you are.*

> *SOMETIMES VS. ALWAYS: When something goes wrong, do you think: "SOMETIMES this happen to me." or do you think: "This ALWAYS happens to me!"*

> *SPECIFIC VS. GLOBAL: Which statement would you most likely find yourself saying? "Math is not my favorite subject when we are practicing division." or "I am terrible at Math. I hate it!"*

**INTRINSIC VS. EXTRINSIC:** Which statement would you most likely find yourself saying? "The words were hard this week. I should have studied more for the test." or "I did really bad on the spelling test. The teacher should not have picked such hard words."

For Grades K-2

Prior to the lesson, make a _thinking stick_ for each "cabin" by attaching laminated cut out copies of the _Thought Bubble_ to sticks or rulers. Have the "campers" in each "cabin" pass around the stick and share their thoughts about different situations with their "cabinmates." Some possible situations for younger students to discuss could be:

You raised your hand, but the teacher didn't call on you.
At lunchtime, a student keeps cutting in front of you in line.
No one seems to want to play with you at recess.
A classmate laughed at you when you dropped your crayon box.

For Grades 3-5

Distribute a copy of _Thinking Situations_ and _What Is Another Way Of Looking At The Situation?_ and paper and pencils to each "cabin." Select one or more students to read aloud the situations one at a time. Have the students in each "cabin" discuss answers for each situation and write these answers on their papers. Allow 2-3 minutes for each "cabin" to complete each situation. _What Is Another Way Of Looking At The Situation?_ suggests possible answers to the last question of each _Thinking Situation_.

Thinking Situations

THINKING SITUATION 1
Some students are in a group giggling, and they are looking your way.

What are you thinking?
What is another way of looking at the situation?

THINKING SITUATION 2
You earned a bad grade on a spelling test.

What are you thinking?
What is another way of looking at the situation?

THINKING SITUATION 3
When your class finally comes out for recess, your best friend is playing with someone else.

What are you thinking?
What is another way of looking at the situation?

THINKING SITUATION 4
Only two kids are able to come to your birthday party this weekend.

What are you thinking?
What is another way of looking at the situation?

THINKING SITUATION 5
Your best friend sends you a "goodnight" text every evening. You didn't receive one last night.

What are you thinking?
What is another way of looking at the situation?

THINKING SITUATION 6
Your ticket hasn't been chosen yet for the Friday prize at school.

What are you thinking?
What is another way of looking at the situation?

THINKING SITUATION 7
You got in trouble for talking in class even though your neighbor was the one who talked first.

What are you thinking?
What is another way of looking at the situation?

THINKING SITUATION 8
You don't understand what's going on in math class. Everyone else says it's super easy.

What are you thinking?
What is another way of looking at the situation?

Camp Care-A-Lot © 2016 Mar★co Products, Inc. 1-800-448-2197

What Is Another Way Of Looking At The Situation?

What is another way of looking at Thinking Situation 1?

Maybe they aren't talking about me. If they are talking about me, they could be sharing something positive they heard about me.

What is another way of looking at Thinking Situation 2?

I should probably study harder next week. I can ask my teacher or parent for ideas about how to work on a few words each night. Maybe I could even ask my teacher if a friend and I could stay in for recess to study the spelling words.

What is another way of looking at Thinking Situation 3?

My friend probably got tired of waiting for my class to come out for recess. I can't expect someone to wait for me without playing. I can go and ask to play with them.

What is another way of looking at Thinking Situation 4?

I'm sure more kids could have come if they had more notice. I sent my invitations out late. It could be a very busy weekend for people.

What is another way of looking at Thinking Situation 5?

I'm sure my BFF got busy or maybe his/her mom or dad wouldn't let him/her call. He/She did say something about going out to eat for his/her Grandmother's birthday. I'm sure he/she is still my best friend.

What is another way of looking at Thinking Situation 6?

There are a lot of students in school who haven't won yet. Maybe I'll win next week.

What is another way of looking at Thinking Situation 7?

I should not have been talking, and I have to take responsibility for my actions. If I am tempted to talk to my neighbor, maybe I should ask to sit somewhere else.

What is another way of looking at Thinking Situation 8?

Just because they are saying it's easy doesn't make it so. It was probably hard for them too, and they are relieved that they understand the assignment. I probably need extra help from the teacher. Maybe I can stay in at recess for help.

Thought Bubble

WHAT'S YOUR MAGIC POTION?

Facilitator's Goal:

To have students review everything talked about in the previous lessons

To have students reflect on their own feelings, then discuss the best strategies to help them in hard times

Materials Needed:

For the facilitator:
- ☐ Table seat assignments
- ☐ Small flashlights for each student group/cabin
- ☐ *Attendance Chart* (page 15 or CD)
- ☐ Lunch supplies
- ☐ Trash can and cleaning supplies
- ☐ Large table or desk
- ☐ Large Mason jar filled about 2/3 full of clear water
- ☐ Food coloring (red, blue, yellow and green),
- ☐ Container of bleach with the words *Magic Potion* written on it
- ☐ Safety glasses and protective gloves

For each student: None

Procedure:

ROLL CALL

Take attendance using the *Attendance Chart*. If some of the students have forgotten to come to *CCAL*, send a reliable student to the cafeteria to check in on them. If they choose not to come, make a note to talk with those students later.

Ask the students to show they are present by replying to the following *Camp Question of the Week.*

At a camp cookout, would you rather eat a hot dog or a hamburger?

REVIEW PROCEDURES

Tell the students:

Lunchroom supplies such as straws, napkins, and utensils are available. Anytime someone feels uncomfortable sharing say, "Pass." This is called our Pass Rule.

What is said in **Camp Care-A-Lot** *stays in* **Camp Care-A-Lot***.*

Treat everyone respectfully.

Any student keeping others from enjoying **Camp Care-A-Lot** *may be asked to leave the group.*

It is necessary that you finish your lunch before the end of the group session.

You need to clean up your "cabins" before you leave.

FLASHLIGHT FEELINGS ACTIVITY (3-5 MINUTES)

If necessary, briefly review how to play *Flashlight Feelings* (see page 13). Then have the students share how their week is going or how they are feeling with other members of their "cabin."

ACTIVITY

Prior to the lesson, place a table/large desk in a part of the room where it is possible for all the students to see it and you. Place the Mason jar filled with clear water, food colorings, and the container of bleach with words *Magic Potion* written on it on the table/desk.

Stand behind the table or desk. Begin the lesson by showing the students the jar of clear water. Then say:

On a great day, when nothing is going wrong, your mind is like this jar of clear water. You can see clearly. Everything is easy to figure out. Your mind is focused and you can think clearly.

However, things happen in life and we experience emotions. I want you to reflect on how you are feeling today, then select one of the colors on the table that best represents that feeling. I will call three or four "campers" at a time to come up to the desk. When you are called, come forward and add no more than a couple drops of your chosen color into the water.

After each student has added food coloring to the water, ask:

Does anyone want to share their reason for selecting the color they did?

Some students will associate positive feelings with a certain color while others will associate negative feelings. Listen to and discuss the reasons for their choices.

Next, hold the jar up at eye level and point out to the students that you can no longer see them clearly through the dark water. Then ask:

What do you do when you can't see clearly?

What helps you get through difficult times?

Then say:

When you encounter difficult times in life, you might experience so many emotions that your judgment becomes clouded and you can't think clearly.

Hold up the container of bleach and say:

This is like a magic potion. We all have different ways of dealing with difficult times. Think about the ways you cope with those times and raise your hand if you would like to share your ideas with the group.

Put on the safety glasses and protective gloves. As each student shares a strategy, pour a little bit of the "magic potion" (liquid bleach) into the container. If not mentioned, include the following strategies:

- Talking with a trusted adult, friend, teacher, counselor, pet
- Journaling or drawing
- Exercising
- Reading books (This is a great time to mention resources you have in your office.)
- Sleeping (Discuss how lack of sleep can affect our ability to think.)
- Taking a walk outside
- Riding a bike
- Keeping a gratitude journal (Make a list of things for which you are thankful.)

As you add the liquid bleach to the water it will become clearer. The water will not become completely clear, it will change to a pale yellowish color.

Say:

By looking at the container we can see that even though the water is much clearer the problem still exists. This is the way it is in life. Our problems are not always completely resolved, but because we have good strategies, we have the ability to think more clearly and make better decisions.

WIENER ROAST

Facilitator's Goal:

To have students celebrate the end of *Camp Care-A-Lot* with their new friends

Materials Needed:

For the facilitator:
- ☐ Hot dogs (one hot dog a piece for K and Grade 1, two hot dogs for Grades 2 and higher)
- ☐ Hot dog buns
- ☐ Ketchup and mustard
- ☐ Chips
- ☐ Cookies (two for each student)
- ☐ Lemonade (lemonade packets may be least expensive)
- ☐ Cups, plates, and napkins
- ☐ Trash can and cleaning supplies
- ☐ Griddle and/or crock pot

Procedure:

The wiener roast is an option that may or may not fit into your schedule. If you feel it would be a beneficial addition to your *CCAL* program, the following pointers could be helpful:

- Determine how you will pay for the event. Possibilities could include PTO money or donations from local businesses.

- It will get very busy, so enlisting parent volunteers or staff members to assist you is helpful.

- You may prefer to host the wiener roast on one day so you don't have set up and clean up more than once. However, it depends on your school's lunch schedules. If the lunch times are staggered, you could keep cooking hot dogs for the next group. A crock pot can also be used to keep the hot dogs warm.

- Communicate with the cafeteria workers as to the number of students that will not be eating in the cafeteria on the dates chosen for the wiener roasts. They will appreciate knowing that less food needs to be prepared.

- Have music or a movie playing to help with crowd control.

- If it's nice outside, the kids could eat outside on the grass.

86

ABOUT THE AUTHOR

Lisa Eck, M.S. has been an elementary school counselor for 18 years in the Indianapolis area. She was 2012 Teacher of The Year. Lisa enjoys public speaking and presented "Counseling In A Crunch" at the 2012 ISCA conference. Prior to school counseling, she was a counselor for emotionally disturbed adolescents in a wilderness, residential treatment center in the piney woods of Texas.

Lisa was raised on a farm in Central Indiana and is now married to a farmer. They raise various crops including corn, soybeans, wheat and tomatoes. But, most importantly they raise their four children. Lisa loves sharing her love for farming with her kids and having them help on the farm. She is also actively involved in her church, loves spending time with her family and friends, and traveling.

INSTRUCTIONS FOR USING THE CD

The CD found inside the back cover provides ADOBE® PDF files of each of the book's reproducible workbook pages, activity sheets, and forms.

The PDFs may be printed in color or grayscale. Choose the appropriate setting on your computer.

These files cannot be modified/edited.

System requirements to open PDF (.pdf) files:

Adobe Reader® 5.0 or newer (compatible with Windows 2000® or newer or Mac OS 9.0® or newer).

THIS CD MAY NOT BE DUPLICATED OR DISTRIBUTED.

PERMISSION TO REPRODUCE: To use the *Camp Care-A-Lot* CD, you must have purchased a copy of the *Camp Care-A-Lot* book. The purchaser may reproduce the book's reproducible activity sheets and forms free and without special permission, for participant use for a particular group or class. **Reproduction of these materials for colleagues, an entire school or school system, or for commercial sale is strictly prohibited.**